# IT'S TIME TO EAT CHERIMOYAS

# It's Time to Eat CHERIMOYAS

Walter the Educator

Silent King Books
A WhichHead Entertainment Imprint

Copyright © 2024 by Walter the Educator

All rights reserved. No part of this book may be reproduced in any manner whatsoever without written per- mission except in the case of brief quotations embodied in critical articles and reviews.

First Printing, 2024

Disclaimer

This book is a literary work; the story is not about specific persons, locations, situations, and/or circumstances unless mentioned in a historical context. Any resemblance to real persons, locations, situations, and/or circumstances is coincidental. This book is for entertainment and informational purposes only. The author and publisher offer this information without warranties expressed or implied. No matter the grounds, neither the author nor the publisher will be accountable for any losses, injuries, or other damages caused by the reader's use of this book. The use of this book acknowledges an understanding and acceptance of this disclaimer.

It's Time to Eat CHERIMOYAS is a collectible early learning book by Walter the Educator suitable for all ages belonging to Walter the Educator's Time to Eat Book Series. Collect more books at WaltertheEducator.com

**USE THE EXTRA SPACE TO TAKE NOTES AND DOCUMENT YOUR MEMORIES**

# CHERIMOYAS

Under the tree, in the warm sunlight,

# It's Time to Eat
# Cherimoyas

It's cherimoya time, oh, what a delight!

With green, bumpy skin, like dragon's scales,

Inside, a treasure of sweet fairy tales.

"Let's cut it open," says Grandpa Lou,

The creamy white flesh is waiting for you.

With seeds like pebbles, shiny and black,

We scoop with a spoon for the perfect snack.

The first little bite melts soft and sweet,

Like candy clouds, it's a dreamy treat.

Banana and pineapple, mango, and pear,

Cherimoya's flavors are beyond compare!

"Pass me a piece!" calls my sister May,

"This fruit is magic, it's made my day!"

She giggles and grins with sticky cheeks,

Cherimoyas bring joy that lasts for weeks.

# It's Time to Eat
# Cherimoyas

We share it plain or blend it smooth,

A tropical shake to brighten the mood.

With every spoonful, the smiles grow,

Cherimoya is the star of the show!

"Remember," says Mom, "don't eat the seeds,

They're not for munching, just the creamy needs!"

We laugh and sort them, one by one,

Eating cherimoyas is so much fun.

On picnics or at the kitchen table,

Cherimoyas make us feel strong and able.

Their fruity goodness fills us with cheer,

A perfect snack throughout the year!

Grandpa says, "In the days of old,

They called this fruit pure 'custard gold.'

A treasure of nature, soft and divine,

# It's Time to Eat
# Cherimoyas

Cherimoyas are simply sublime."

As the sun sets low, we finish our treat,

The cherimoya snack is oh so sweet.

We save a few seeds to plant and grow,

For more cherimoyas in tomorrow's glow.

So let's give thanks for this fruit so fine,

Cherimoyas, oh how they shine!

A creamy dream, a fruity cheer,

# It's Time to Eat
# Cherimoyas

The sweetest treat to share each year!

# ABOUT THE CREATOR

Walter the Educator is one of the pseudonyms for Walter Anderson. Formally educated in Chemistry, Business, and Education, he is an educator, an author, a diverse entrepreneur, and he is the son of a disabled war veteran. "Walter the Educator" shares his time between educating and creating. He holds interests and owns several creative projects that entertain, enlighten, enhance, and educate, hoping to inspire and motivate you. Follow, find new works, and stay up to date with Walter the Educator™

at WaltertheEducator.com

www.ingramcontent.com/pod-product-compliance
Lightning Source LLC
LaVergne TN
LVHW010622070526
838199LV00063BA/5243